Good Thoughts

Good Words   *Good Deeds*

Zarathustra

The Influence of the Persian
Prophet on Nietzsche's Philosophy

By Bahram Moterassed (Spitama)

© Copyright 2025 by Bahram Moterassed (Spitama)

All rights reserved.

The content contained within this book may not be reproduced, duplicated, or transmitted without direct written permission from the author or the publisher.

Under no circumstances will any blame or legal responsibility be held against the publisher or author for any damages, reparation, or monetary loss due to the information contained within this book, either directly or indirectly.

ISBN: 978-1-0689768-6-5 (Hardcover)
        978-1-0689768-5-8 (Paperback)
        978-1-0689768-7-2 (Ebook)

Table of Contents

About the Author v

Introduction: Nietzsche's revelation vii

    Zarathustra is not a fictional character vii

    The Inner Voice *(Seraôša)* xii

    The Purpose of The Book xv

Chapter 1: Zarathustra's Enlightenment 1

    Zarathustra's Solitude 1

    The Metaphor of Sun 4

    Ancient Persian Savior: Mithra 5

    The Spiritual Sun 7

    Metaphor of Eagle and Serpent 12

    Zarathustra: The Shining Star 16

Chapter 2: Zarathustra's down-going 19

    Meeting the Monk 19

    Life Affirming 21

    God is Dead 25

    "Willpower" is not "will to power" 30

Chapter 3: Zarathustra's Philosophy 35

    The God Within 35

The Twin Spirits: Unity, Not Duality 36
Ahriman (Evil) 39
Hell and Heaven 40
Beyond Good and Evil... 42
The Choice Is Yours 43
Two Sides of a Coin... 44
Conscience (*Daenâ*): The Inner Morality 45
Our Higher Being 47

Chapter 4: Übermensch: A Transformation of Humanity Toward Wisdom and Consciousness............................ 49
Progressive Mentality (*Vohuman*)............................ 51
Existing vs. Living 55
Übermensch: A Conscious and Wise Human Being . 58
The Magi 62
Eternal Recurrence.. 66
Zarathustra's Despair 68

Conclusion 73

About the Author

BAHRAM MOTERASSED (Spitama)[1] has been a psychotherapist for thirty years, incorporating Eastern spirituality into his practice. He has a BA in psychology and a master's degree in marriage and family therapy. He has studied and practiced Sufism, Buddhism, Yoga, Mazdaism, Christianity, Kabbalah, and sweat lodges. He has also practiced and taught meditation courses for more than thirty years. Bahram is the author of Born to Fly, You Are Beyond Who You Are, Good Thoughts, Good Words, Good Deeds, and Your Immortal Spirit: From Death to Deathlessness, and The Messiah: Saoshyant.

www.zarathustra.ca

---

1 Spitama is chosen here because of the author's immense love and respect for the wisdom of Zarathustra Spitama.

INTRODUCTION
Nietzsche's revelation

Zarathustra is not a fictional character

Many people believe that Zarathustra, the character in Nietzsche's *Thus Spoke Zarathustra*, is fictional. However, it is important to know that Nietzsche was well aware of the history and philosophy of this great ancient Persian and Indo-European prophet. In his notes, Nietzsche expressed great respect for him. He had a deeper connection with Zarathustra than just seeing him as a fictional character of his creation. By naming his book after Zarathustra, he honored the prophet while also using him to share his philosophy.

In doing so, he made Zarathustra an important part of his philosophy. Zarathustra's teachings offer deep wisdom for those who seek to understand themselves and the world. He expressed his connection with the prophet, saying, *Before Zarathustra, there was no wisdom, no probing of the soul, no art of speech.*[2] Nietzsche was inspired to share this light and wisdom with humanity.

Zarathustra lived about 5000 years ago in Persia (modern-day Iran). His mission was to introduce a concept of God and religion that was different from the beliefs that dominated his time. He did not intend to entangle the human spirit with superstition or robotic rituals. On the contrary, he dreamt of breaking the chains of ignorance that kept humanity imprisoned in unconsciousness and deception. His vision was fundamentally about inner growth and self-realization.

Zarathustra did not want people to follow him blindly. In contrast, he intended to empower individuals to actively increase their consciousness toward the Divine Consciousness. He challenged us to look at ourselves not as who we are but as who we can become. His aim for humanity was for us to transcend to become higher, conscious beings. And those higher human beings are

---

[2] Nietzsche, Friedrich. Ecce Homo: How One Becomes What One Is. Translated by Dr. Oscar Levy, The Macmillan Company, 1911, p. 107

hidden within us. We are like a ladder. We need to climb up the steps of our beings in order to reach the treasure of our full consciousness. Then, we are not human anymore. We become closer to God, Ahura Mazda—the Ultimate Consciousness, the Supreme Wisdom.

His philosophy eventually established Zoroastrianism as the dominant religion in Persia. It remained the state religion of the empire until about the seventh century (CE) when Muslims conquered Persia. Throughout history, Zarathustra's wisdom has had a profound influence on various cultures and belief systems. It shaped the philosophical and religious thought of ancient Greece, with figures such as Pythagoras, Socrates, and Plato drawing inspiration from his teachings.

Zarathustra's influence on Western culture can be seen in literature and philosophy impacting figures like Dante, Voltaire, and Nietzsche. In the 19th century, European scholarship on Zoroastrianism grew. The French linguist Anquetil-Duperron translated the *Gathas*, Zarathustra's sublime songs, into modern language in the late 18th century. This made Zarathustra's wisdom and philosophy available for the first time in centuries. The translation made him an important figure and a pioneer in the understanding of ancient religions. Nietzsche, as a scholar of ancient languages, studied Greek and Latin texts that mentioned Zarathustra. The ancient Greeks and Romans admired Zoroaster as a wise figure. Philosophers like Herodotus, Plato, and Pliny wrote about Zarathustra's mystical and religious ideas, which likely influenced Nietzsche's thinking.

Nietzsche saw Zarathustra as an awakened person who challenged traditional beliefs and questioned established values. Zarathustra's approach aligned with Nietzsche's philosophy. Similarly, he also questioned societal norms and the herd mentality. Just as Nietzsche criticized the dominant religion of his time, Zarathustra confronted the hypocrisy of the priests during his life. Both figures aimed to inspire individuals to think for themselves and seek deeper truths beyond societal approval. Nietzsche viewed his Zarathustra as someone who could challenge traditional morality and values in pursuit of a higher purpose.

Nietzsche's sister, Elisabeth Förster-Nietzsche, wrote a lot about her brother's life and works, including *Thus Spoke Zarathustra*. In her introductions and commentaries, she shares her thoughts on Nietzsche's deep interest in the ancient Persian prophet Zarathustra (Zoroaster). She stated that Nietzsche saw Zarathustra as a transformative figure in human history. Elisabeth said that her brother was fascinated by Zarathustra's teachings and his important role in shaping morality, which influenced many religious and ethical systems.

She stated that *My brother had the figure of Zarathustra in his mind from a very early age. He once told me that even as a child, he dreamed of him. At different times in his life, he referred to this figure by various names. In the end, however, he honored the Persian heritage by identifying him with this creature of my imagination. The Persians were the first to take a broad view of history. According to them, every series of evolutions was guided by a prophet, and each prophet had his own Hazar, a dynasty lasting a thousand years. All of Zarathustra's ideas, as well as his personality, were early concepts in my brother's mind.³*

The Inner Voice *(Seraôša)*

Writing *Thus Spoke Zarathustra* was a deep and almost mystical experience for Nietzsche. He described it as a revelation that came to him with great power. He expressed it as something beyond just normal inspiration or thought. He felt as if he were in a state of ecstasy, totally out of his control. He stated his experience while writing the book, saying, *During those moments when my creative energy flowed most plentifully, my muscular activity was always greatest. The body is inspired: let us waive the question of 'soul.' I often found myself dancing... able to walk for seven or eight hours without fatigue.*⁴ He was inspired to write about Zarathustra's wisdom at those moments.

---

3 Friedrich Nietzsche, Thus Spoke Zarathustra, trans. Thomas Common (New York: Modern Library, 1909), Introduction by Mrs. Förster-Nietzsche.
4 Nietzsche, Friedrich. *Ecce Homo: How One Becomes What One Is*. Translated by Dr. Oscar Levy, The Macmillan Company, 1911, p. 104-105.

Nietzsche described this state as a revelation. Thoughts, metaphors, and rhythms came to him in flashes. It felt as if Zarathustra had come to him, speaking through him with little effort. He said, *It was on these two roads that all Zarathustra came to me, above all, Zarathustra himself as a type-I ought rather to say that it was on these walks that **he waylaid me**.*[5]

Nietzsche's revelations and the force that he experienced were not only intellectual. They felt powerful, mystical, and almost supernatural, affecting his whole being. Whether supernatural or not, his experience was similar to a deep spiritual transformation. He described his inspiration, saying, *At the time, few understood true inspiration. Some saw themselves as mere vessels of a higher power. Revelation comes suddenly, with certainty—'thoughts flash like lightning—inevitable and unchosen.' In moments of ecstasy, one is swept away, both strong and vulnerable. Tears may flow, energy surges, and*

---

[5] Ibid., 99.

even sorrow deepens the joy. Everything occurs spontaneously, as if born from a divine wellspring.[6]

Zarathustra refers to this kind of intuition or inner voice - *Seraôša*. It represents the divine voice emerging to us from *Vohuman* (good mind). Zarathustra advises us to follow the voice of the Supreme Wisdom (Ahura Mazda) and to follow *Seraôša*, which is the voice of conscience. It is also known as the voice of intuition. Intuition means listening carefully to the voices of our spirit and heart in order to guide us toward the conscious path.

In Zarathustra's teaching, *Seraôša* acts as a channel through which divine truth becomes available to the individual. This process of tuning ourselves to the sacred inner source is similar to adjusting a radio in order to receive the clearest message from the main source. When one is attuned to *Seraôša or* voice of intuition, the individual becomes receptive to the guidance of conscience and with divine wisdom.

---

6 Ibid., 101-102

> *Grant me, O Mazda, the strength and insight to fully grasp and follow the path of Asha through Seraôša's guiding presence. May I listen and discern with clarity, dedicating my mind and actions to uphold Truth. Let Seraôša dwell within me so that I may remain unwavering in my devotion to your teachings, aligning my life with your divine order.[7]*

By listening to intuition (*Seraôša*), one connects with the divine. *Seraôša* bridges the human and divine worlds, bringing clarity to the many voices within us—cultural, familial, and societal influences that we carry throughout our lives. It guides us toward truth and wisdom, freeing us from harmful thoughts. In the *Gathas*, *Seraôša* plays a key role, guiding Zarathustra to his revelation and inspiring his sacred verses. Similarly, Nietzsche's revelation came when he was overtaken by an inner voice, directing him to write *Thus Spoke Zarathustra*.

The Purpose of The Book

It's unfortunate that Nietzsche's interpretation of Zarathustra has often been misunderstood and misused.

---

[7] Gathas, Yasna 35.5-6

Thus, Spoke Zarathustra intended to challenge traditional values and encourage personal growth. However, some have twisted his ideas to support nihilism or other harmful beliefs, which was not Nietzsche's intent. Many of his deeper ideas have been lost or misrepresented, leading to interpretations that miss the true essence of his philosophy and Zarathustra's original teachings. Zarathustra's message emphasizes wisdom, responsibility, and moral clarity. These are all important aspects for both personal and societal growth.

This book aims to explore the ideas presented in *Thus Spoke Zarathustra* through the lens of the ancient teachings of the prophet Zarathustra and the rich culture of Persia. Nietzsche was deeply influenced by these teachings to explore his own philosophical concepts. Understanding the historical and cultural context is key to gaining a deeper understanding of both Zarathustra and Nietzsche within a more meaningful framework.

By examining the spiritual and ethical dimensions of Zarathustra, we can gain a clearer understanding of how Nietzsche interpreted the ancient Persian spiritual view.

This exploration will show how Zarathustra's teachings on wisdom, morality, and human potential connect with Nietzsche's philosophy. It will help readers understand his ideas and inspire those seeking wisdom and personal transformation.

Zarathustra emphasizes the importance of consciousness, free will, and living by *good thoughts, good words, and good deeds*, which are essential for spiritual growth. He encourages us to connect with a higher purpose and make conscious choices that reflect wisdom and integrity. Zarathustra's message emphasizes that true freedom and growth come from expanding our awareness. It requires rising above our lower desires and connecting with the Divine consciousness. Zarathustra's unique contribution is his strong call for individuals to take responsibility for their choices. He has encouraged humanity to actively shape their own lives and destiny.

It is important to emphasize that this book is rooted in the esoteric teachings of Zarathustra, which were preserved and passed down by the Magi after his death. The Magi, the ancient priestly class, were spiritual leaders and guardians of Zarathustra's deeper wisdom. They were responsible for establishing the path of Mazda-Yasna, meaning "the followers of wisdom" or "the worshipers of wisdom." This tradition is different from the more formalized religious practices of Zoroastrianism which later became the dominant religion of the Persian Empire for over a thousand years. The focus of Mazda-Yasna was not on ritual or dogma, but on cultivating inner wisdom, personal transformation, and conscious living.

This book explores the inner meaning of Zarathustra's teachings, offering a profound exploration of how his guidance can help us expand our consciousness. Rather than focusing on external religious practices or the historical evolution of Zoroastrianism, this work seeks to unveil the spiritual essence of Zarathustra's message. The teachings within Mazda-Yasna emphasize the importance of inner growth, self-awareness, and aligning oneself with the divine principles of wisdom and truth, principles. This approach closely aligns with Nietzsche's philosophy as presented in his book *Thus Spoke Zarathustra*.

CHAPTER 1

Zarathustra's Enlightenment

Zarathustra's Solitude

> *When Zarathustra was thirty years old, he left his home and the lake of his home, and went into the mountains. There he enjoyed his spirit and his solitude, and for ten years did not weary of it.*[8]

Nietzsche was well aware of Zarathustra's age when he became enlightened. He was thirty years old when he received his revelation. Mary Boyce, a Zoroastrian scholar, stated that, a*ccording to tradition, Zoroaster was thirty, the time of ripe wisdom, when revelation finally came to him.*[9] As Nietzsche described in his book, the

---

[8] Friedrich Nietzsche, Thus Spoke Zarathustra, trans. Thomas Common (New York: Modern Library, 1909), 3.

[9] Mary Boyce, *Zoroastrians: Their Religious Beliefs and Practices* (London: Routledge & Kegan Paul, 1979), 19.

prophet sought to retreat into the mountains for contemplation and connection with his inner world. According to Dhalla, another scholar of Zoroastrianism, Zarathustra went to the mountains to be in solitude in order to connect with his inner being. *Mountains lift their heads majestically on the Iranian plateau, and Zarathushtra retreated into the mountain fastness. Here, far removed from the stress and strife of life, and with no human sound to distract his thoughts, he made his home.*[10]

The songs in the Gathas[11] are Zarathustra's inner dialogue with his inner wisdom. He did not see the Sublime Wisdom (Ahura Mazda) outside himself, but within. We misunderstand Zarathustra's teachings completely if we reduce them to a dialogue with a being outside of himself. The wisdom he found was through his inner voice (*Seraôša*) and inner ears.

> *As I have perceived Ahura Mazda with my inner sight,* I will strive to draw His attention toward me through songs of praise. Having realized, through good thoughts, words, and deeds, as well as through

---

[10] Dhalla, *History of Zoroastrianism* (New York: Oxford University Press, 1938), 14.
[11] Zarathustra's sublime songs

honesty and integrity, that Ahura Mazda is the Lord of Life and Wisdom, the sole Creator of the World, I will offer Him my sincere praise with full devotion.[12]

In this context, Zarathustra is not speaking about physical sight, but the awakening of one's inner consciousness, which allows the recognition of the divine and truth. The "inner eyes" are the faculties of perception beyond the physical senses. They represent the ability to perceive deeper spiritual truths. Zarathustra was like a diver who searched in the depths of the ocean to find a pearl. He dove into the depths of his own consciousness to find that pearl of wisdom (Mazda) within. The real self is nothing more than Mazda.

However, Nietzsche added ten years to the age of Zarathustra's revelation. He used age 40 metaphorically as the number of completion and maturation. The number 40 is significant in many spiritual traditions. For instance, the Jews wandered in the hardship of the desert for 40 years before reaching the promised land. Similarly, Yeshua (Jesus in Greek) fasted for 40 days in the desert to prepare

---

12 Gathas, Yasna 45.8

himself for his mission. In both of these examples, the number 40 symbolizes a time of testing, growth, and eventual spiritual fulfillment. Nietzsche used it metaphorically to represent Zarathustra's journey toward ultimate wisdom and spiritual maturity.

The Metaphor of Sun

But eventually, his heart changed, and one morning, rising with the rosy dawn, he went before the sun and spoke to it:

O great star, what would your happiness be if you did not have those for whom you shine? For ten years, you have climbed up to my cave; You would not have worn off your light and of the journey, had it not been for me, my eagle, and my serpent. But we awaited you every morning, took from you your overflow, and blessed you for it.[13]

Nietzsche understood the significance of the sun as a metaphor in Persian culture and Zarathustra's teachings

---

13 Friedrich Nietzsche, Thus Spoke Zarathustra, trans. Thomas Common (New York: Modern Library, 1909).

when he wrote this part. Before Zarathustra's revelation, the Persians worshipped Mithra, the Sun God. In fact, Zarathustra was initially a priest in Mithra's temple and came from a family with a long tradition of priesthood in Mithraic tradition. However, Zarathustra later opposed the Mithraic path, its rituals, and other Persian deities such as Anahita, Bahram, and Vayu. He introduced a new spiritual vision centered on Ahura Mazda and the principles of truth and wisdom.

Ancient Persian Savior: Mithra

Traditionally, the ancient Persians worshipped a multitude of gods and goddesses. Among them was Mithra, the god of the rising sun, who played a central role in Persian spirituality. Mithra was seen as the protector of people in order to bring justice and order on Earth. It was believed that Mithra took on human form while preserving his divine nature. He came to Earth to guide humanity toward the true path.

The name *Mithra* comes from the root *mihr*, meaning both "friend" and "contract." The Sun, represented by

Mithra, was not only seen as a source of light but also as a Creator, Ruler, Preserver, and Savior of the world. Without its light and warmth, life on Earth would not exist. Thus, Mithra was considered the Savior who brought life, light, and warmth to humanity.

Mithra was also viewed as the protector of truth and justice, revealing everything to humanity, dispelling darkness, and lifting ignorance. The day dedicated to him, Sunday (Sun-Day), was a special occasion to honor his divine presence. There was an exchange in the relationship: while Mithra was the Creator and Savior of people, they were expected to honor and worship him in return.

For over 7,000 years in Persia, Mithra's birthday was celebrated on December 22. The term "Yalda" means "birth" and marks both Mithra's birth and the Winter Solstice. Yalda is still celebrated in Iran today and is linked with the birth of the Savior, Mithra, symbolizing the victory of light over darkness. This celebration occurs around December 21, the longest night of the year, signaling the start of longer days as the sun (Mithra, the

Savior) is "born" again. It signifies the sun's return and the lengthening of days.

The Spiritual Sun

In Zarathustra's teachings, Ahura Mazda (The Supreme Being/Spirit) is likened to the spiritual sun. It is the ultimate source of all existence. Just as the sun is essential for life on Earth, Ahura Mazda is the Original Being from which everything in the universe originates. Everything, both seen and unseen, is part of this Divine Energy. Our lives are not separate from this source; we are deeply connected to it.

The sun and fire are central symbols in Zarathustra's teachings, representing the light of creation, consciousness, wisdom, and the energy of action. Zarathustra's path is not one of blind obedience to scripture but of *inner illumination.* It is an awareness and consciousness that must burn continuously, bringing light both within and without. Just as the sun shines without external validation, true wisdom and consciousness must radiate from within. It needs no external authority to prove their existence.

As the sun's rays give light and warmth to the planets, Ahura Mazda also gives the rays of love and wisdom to existence unconditionally. If it is a sunny day and we are sitting in a dark basement, it does not mean that the sun is withholding its light and warmth from us. We just need to get out to where the sun shines. Depending on our level of maturity and our closeness to Ahura Mazda, we will receive more, or less, love and wisdom. As the sun radiates light and warmth to the darkness and coldness of Earth and brings life to it, Ahura Mazda also radiates life to every living being and to the darkness of our ignorance and unconsciousness. As the light of Earth cannot exist without the sun, there is no life apart from the illumination of The Supreme Being.

Figure #1. **The Spiritual Sun**

Zarathustra teaches that individuals must cultivate this inner light. One needs to maintain a state of awareness that allows them to act spontaneously in every situation. People do not need to follow rigid laws but by their own awakened wisdom. The sun burns with its own energy and lights up everything without discrimination. In Zoroastrian tradition, prayers are directed toward the sun, not as an object of worship, but as a symbol of Ahura Mazda, the Supreme Wisdom. Like Ahura Mazda, the sun doesn't demand obedience but offers light freely, allowing everyone to see and act in truth.

> *Those who, with their minds and actions, uphold Truth (Asha) and wisdom shall receive the blessings of Ahura Mazda. Their souls shall be strengthened by the flame of righteousness, and they shall walk the path of divine light. But those who choose the Lie (Druj) shall be far from this grace.*[14]

In Zarathustra's description, the analogy of light representing consciousness is significant. Light not only reveals itself but also illuminates its surroundings. For instance, when there is a burning candle in a dark room, the candle not only illuminates its own existence but also reveals everything around it. Similarly, the sun does not require anything else to prove its existence. Its light is evidence of its being, and it also brings to light whatever is hidden in the darkness. In a dark room, a bookshelf would not be visible without the candlelight. The bookshelf relies on the candlelight to be seen, but the candlelight itself does not need the shelf or anything else to be visible. Its own illumination is proof of its existence.

---

[14] Gathas: Yasna 34.4

> *Through the highest wisdom, O Ahura, those who uphold Truth with their words and deeds shall be radiant in Your light. But those who turn away from wisdom and righteousness shall dwell in darkness, far from Your blessings.*[15]

Just as the moon has no light of its own and only shines through the illumination of the sun, human beings do not possess their own consciousness in isolation. It is only by opening ourselves to the Light of Supreme Wisdom that we can truly shine and radiate. Without this Light, we remain in the darkness of our ignorance, unable to see, act, or truly live.

Nietzsche, inspired by this rich Persian and Zoroastrian tradition, adopted the sun as a powerful symbol in *Thus Spoke Zarathustra*. He used it to illustrate the journey of self-overcoming, personal transformation, and the pursuit of higher consciousness. His understanding of this cultural and philosophical symbol is reflected in his work, demonstrating his respect for the sun metaphor in Zarathustra's teachings.

---

[15] Gathas: Yasna 31.13

Metaphor of Eagle and Serpent

You would not have worn off your light and of the journey, had it not been for me, my eagle, and my serpent. But we awaited you every morning, took from you your overflow, and blessed you for it.[16]

In Nietzsche's book, two animals symbolize the teachings of Zarathustra: the snake and the eagle.

Snakes are not seen as evil or deceitful in many spiritual traditions. Snake is an animal of transformation. There comes a point in a snake's life that the snake needs to grow larger. The old skin is too tight. The snake begins to shed off the old skin and creates a bigger skin to fit the grown body. Similarly, when we get to a point that the old ways and patterns in our lives become tight for us or are restricting us, we need to create a new skin of characters and patterns in our lives. Like the snake shedding off the old skin, we also need to get rid of negative energy in order to let a healthier person grow.

---

16 Friedrich Nietzsche, Thus Spoke Zarathustra

The **eagle** is a metaphor for our higher consciousness. The eagle flies high above the earth. It is the perfect symbol for the awakened soul. It is the soul that has embraced wisdom and risen beyond the illusions of the lower self. It is the symbol of Zoroastrian religion. In Zoroastrianism, *Faravashi*, the human with eagle-like wings, represents this divine ascent, the flight toward our ultimate being.

Figure #2. ***Faravashi***
A human with two wings flying like an eagle,
indicates that our purpose in life is to ascend from our lowest animalistic level to a higher consciousness.

The eagle does not crawl on the ground. It spreads its wings and rises to the depth of the sky. An eagle is like the awakened person who embraces truth and rises above his illusions. From above, the eagle sees what those stuck below cannot. This is the power of consciousness. It is to lift ourselves higher and see beyond superficial understanding. When we awaken to the light within, we grow wings and fly like an eagle. We see clearly, similar to an eagle's eyesight. We can distinguish falsehood from truth. To be conscious is to fly—to live like the eagle. This is Zarathustra's path. It is a journey of ascending high like an eagle from our lower selves to our highest potential as a human being. It is a path to rise from our fears and illusion into divine wisdom.

Before one can fly like an eagle and to be a conscious human being, one must first transform. In Persian tradition, the snake (*mar*) is the symbol of transformation, of shedding the old and embracing the new. Just as a snake sheds its skin, we must let go of our past selves to grow into our conscious being. In both Zoroastrian and Hindu traditions, the snake represents vital energy—what Hindus call *Kundalini*. In Persian, when a person is sick, they are said to have low vital energy—low *mar* (snake). The word *Bimar* (بیمار, ill, sick) means "without the snake," without the inner force that sustains life. A hospital (*Bimaristan*) is where those with weakened life energy go to regain their strength. To rise like the eagle, we must first transform like the snake. We must shed fear, illusion, and ignorance, embracing the conscious self within.

Nietzsche uses the eagle and the serpent as symbols to explain the journey to enlightenment. The serpent represents the awakening of our inner energy and the process of transformation. The eagle represents the higher consciousness that comes after that transformation. In *Zarathustra*, Nietzsche shows that to reach a higher state of awareness; we must first awaken and transform ourselves like the serpent shedding its skin. Then, we are able to rise, like the eagle, and see life from a higher perspective. Zarathustra himself is both the serpent and the eagle. He has undergone transformation, shedding his old self and rising as a conscious being to guide others toward awakening. He has reached a point where he is full of wisdom and love for all living beings. Like a bee full of honey, he shares his wisdom.

> *Behold, I am weary of my wisdom, like the bee that has gathered too much honey; I need hands outstretched to receive it. I long to give and distribute, until the wise once again find joy in their folly, and the poor find happiness in their abundance.*

> *Therefore, I must descend into the depths, as you do in the evening when you sink behind the sea, casting your light also on the underworld, you radiant star! Just as you descend, so must I, to those to whom I will go.*[17]

Zarathustra: The Shining Star

Zarathustra was the title given to him after his enlightenment. "Zar" means gold (*zar* in Persian), and "ushtra" means light or star (ستاره in Persian). Zarathustra, therefore, means "the shining star" or "the one who possesses the Golden Light." Nietzsche understood the meaning behind the prophet's name. Zarathustra had reached a state where he was no longer searching for light—he had become light itself. Like the sun, he illuminated wisdom. He became Zarathustra, the shining star. His time had come to descend from his solitude, just as the sun set. He was downgoing to share his illumination with those still in darkness.

Zarathustra leaves his mountain retreat to share his wisdom with humanity. Like the sun that gives life and

---

[17] Friedrich Nietzsche, Thus Spoke Zarathustra

clarity to the world, he descends to awaken others. His aim is not to impose himself on others but to inspire them to find truth in their own paths. His wisdom, like the sun's light, does not command. He goes down to nurture people, helping them reveal their highest self.

Zarathustra's descent is not a fall, but a deliberate act of bringing light where there is darkness. He invited people on a journey of self-transformation, calling others to rise and to shine with a light of their own. Zarathustra is a gardener, encouraging us to plant the seed of our existence so that we may bloom into higher consciousness. He does not see us as caterpillars; he sees in each of us the potential to become butterflies.

Zarathustra is not here to impose himself on us; rather, he is a loving father, a teacher, and a guide who gathers us under the same roof despite our differences. He is not a "guru," but an alarm clock awakening us to the dawn of our true existence. Like a rooster crowing at sunrise, he calls us to wake from our deep sleep. He does not ask for followers—he does not need them. Instead, he urges you to follow your own intelligence, your own wisdom, and your own consciousness.

> *Bless me, then, you tranquil eye, that can look upon the greatest happiness without envy! Bless this cup about to overflow, so its waters may pour out like gold, spreading the reflection of your joy everywhere.*
>
> *Look! This cup is about to empty once more, and Zarathustra will become a man again.*
>
> *Thus began Zarathustra's down-going.*[18]

---

[18] Friedrich Nietzsche, Thus Spoke Zarathustra

CHAPTER 2

Zarathustra's down-going

Meeting the Monk

On his way down from the mountain cave, Zarathustra meets a saint living in the forest removed from the world. The saint spends his time meditating, dancing, singing, and contemplating God. He finds peace in his solitude. He lives alone, believing that separation from the world brings him closer to divine understanding. The saint notices a change in Zarathustra, which is something different about his presence. He asks why Zarathustra has left his isolation.

Zarathustra responds that he has come down because of his love for humanity. He wants to share his wisdom with the people. He intends to help them awaken to a new way of living. He wants to free people from their limited beliefs. However, the saint does not agree with Zarathustra's approach. He doesn't want to help mankind.

He sees humanity as too imperfect and weak to be helped. To the saint, people are lost and beyond saving. He insists that Zarathustra should not go down and try to share his wisdom with them. He warns that the people will not understand Zarathustra and will reject him. The saint encourages him to stay in his solitude and focus only on his connection with God rather than awakening the imperfect humanity.

The saint believes that the path of isolation is the only true path. He sees the people as unworthy of Zarathustra's wisdom and advises him to turn away from the world. He suggests to Zarathustra to retreat back into the safety of his cave and to contemplate on God alone.

Zarathustra, however, is not convinced. He sees the saint's view as limited, clinging to the old ideas of separation and detachment from humanity. Zarathustra knows that his mission is to bring light to the people, even if they do not yet understand it. He is well aware that the journey of transformation begins with the courage to face challenges. The path is an individual's growth of consciousness and upliftment of others even if it involves rejection and danger in his life.

Life Affirming

Zarathustra didn't support a revolution. Instead, he encouraged us to go through an evolution and change from within. A revolution is about changing external systems of government, while evolution happens inside us. It is about growing from ignorance to consciousness. It is about how aware and wise we are. Every revolution, from Spartacus to Marxism and Socialism, has not succeeded. That is because the people who took over after the old system were just as unconscious as those before them.

Zarathustra came to bring higher consciousness so that people can live based on their own inner conscience (Daenâ), not on the higher ethical codes imposed upon them. Unlike everything else in the universe, human beings are unique because they are designed to grow and develop themselves. This sets us apart from all other forms of creation. Humans are like unfinished buildings—works in progress. Each person has the responsibility to take charge of their own growth, striving to become more conscious and wise. This is the true purpose of life on Earth: to complete ourselves and to rise to a higher state of being.

Zarathustra did not preach against the pleasures of life or renouncing the world. He was not an ascetic, nor did he promote self-denial, self-inflicted suffering, or isolation. Unlike many religious figures, he did not call for his followers to withdraw from society, remain celibate, or reject the material world. Instead, he was an awakened human being whose mission was to awaken others. He believed that the spiritual path and inner growth happen not in solitude but in connection with others and within the community. His teachings emphasize joy, gratitude for existence, and active participation in the world rather than withdrawal from it.

> *Ahura Mazda, the Supreme Ruler, has declared that true fortune is reserved for those who bring happiness to others. The one who helps others find peace and fulfillment, For in the service of others, the*

soul finds its true path, And in giving, one receives the greatest of blessings.[19]

Zarathustra was deeply troubled by the cruelty and recklessness of humanity toward each other and destruction of nature and earth. He recognized that true spirituality requires responsibility, not only toward oneself but toward the world as a whole. To walk the path of consciousness and Light is to protect and honor life. It is about to act as a guardian of the earth rather than a destroyer. Only through conscious effort, we can align ourselves with divine wisdom and fulfill our purpose on earth.

Unto You, O Ahura Mazda, the Soul of Creation cried out in distress: "Why did You fashion me? Who has given me over to suffering and oppression? None but You have I as a protector; grant me a savior, a guide who will stand for righteousness and deliver me from harm."[20]

---

[19] Gathas: Yasna 43.1
[20] Gathas: Yasna 29.1

Indeed, Zarathustra was chosen to descend among us and to awaken us for his love, purity, and wisdom. He came among us to illuminate the path toward a conscious and loving humanity.

> *Then Ahura Mazda, with the wisdom of the Good Mind, asked: "Who is willing to be the protector and savior of this world, to stand against falsehood and uphold truth?' Then, O Zarathustra, you were chosen as the one who would accept this task. Among all, you were found to be the most righteous, the one whose soul was most devoted to Asha (Truth based on Harmony and Balance)."* [21]

And, he accepted the invitation to bring his wisdom, joy, and awakening to the world.

> *With humble adoration, I extend my hands in prayer to You, O Mazda! Grant me, through Your Holy Spirit, all righteousness in my actions and all wisdom of the Good Mind, so that I may bring joy to the Soul of Creation.* [22]

---

[21] Gathas: Yasna 29.6
[22] Gathas: Yasna 28.1

God is Dead

When Zarathustra was alone, however, he said to his heart: "Could it be possible! This old saint in the forest has not yet heard of it, that God is dead!"[23]

One of the greatest misconceptions about Nietzsche's statement "God is dead" is the assumption that he was promoting nihilism or atheism. In reality, his message goes much deeper. Nietzsche was not denying the existence of God; he was challenging the traditional concept of God. He recognized that humanity had outgrown the old religious frameworks. Nietzsche's declaration that "God is dead" was not a rejection of religious belief. Rather, it was an invitation for people to embrace their own strength and take responsibility for their destiny. He encouraged individuals to actively shape their future instead of being passive participants.

Zarathustra's teachings were revolutionary for the same reason. Before him, people believed that their lives and destinies were controlled by many gods and goddesses.

---

23 Friedrich Nietzsche, Thus Spoke Zarathustra

They lived as their fate was not on their own efforts. However, under Zarathustra's influence, a new understanding evolved. He placed human beings at the center of their own destiny. He taught that we are not powerless in the hands of divine forces but rather the masters of our own choices and actions.

> *O Mazda, through Your perfect wisdom, You created us with both physical bodies and spiritual awareness. By Your divine Thought, You granted us the ability to think, speak, and act, allowing us the freedom to choose our own destiny according to our will.*[24]

Nietzsche saw in Zarathustra the first great thinker who challenged humanity to turn away from blind obedience to gods, gurus, or masters who seek to dominate us. Zarathustra's message was not rooted in misery, pain, or despair. He saw goodness in each of us that needed to be nurtured and empowered. He encouraged us to take responsibility for our own lives, seek wisdom, and create meaning through our will and actions. In this way, both

---

[24] Gathas: Yasna 31.11

Zarathustra and Nietzsche rejected passive faith and called for an active, creative effort in our lives.

> *Listen with your ears to the highest truth, Reflect on it with enlightened minds, And let each person choose their own path, For in this freedom, one shapes their destiny.*[25]

Zarathustra introduced the concepts of willpower and freedom of choice, which were revolutionary in a world where most people believed their destinies were controlled by a few. His ideas were foreign to many, as only a privileged few had control over the lives of others. The majority lived in poverty, slavery, or under rigid social structures that left them with little to no control over their future.

Zarathustra's teachings challenged this passive mindset about 5,000 years ago. He taught that human beings are not powerless. We are not puppets of the gods, but active participants in shaping our own destiny. He called on people to rise above their circumstances and live with a higher purpose. He sought to empower everyone to

---

[25] Gathas: Yasna 30.3

use their ability to choose between truth and falsehood, wisdom and ignorance.

In a world where suffering and hardship are unavoidable, Zarathustra's teaching about personal responsibility and self-determination was revolutionary. He did not promise an escape from life and hardships. Rather, he encouraged people not to submit to their fates. He taught us that through our own will and effort, we could rise above our limitations and become masters of our own lives.

Nietzsche recognized the profound impact of Zarathustra's teachings. In *Thus Spoke Zarathustra*, he presents a figure who challenges us to break free from our slavery. He awakens us to find our own strength within. This is the essence of Zarathustra's message: the power to create one's own fate lies not in the hands of gods but in the will of every individual.

> *May we be like those who work to advance the world toward perfection. May Mazda and the Divine Spirits support and guide our efforts through Truth. For it*

is in the mind of a conscious person that Wisdom truly resides.[26]

As the flame of any fire rises, human beings should strive to improve themselves in order to progress in life. From Zarathustra's perspective, the relationship between Ahura Mazda and humans is not one of child to parent, nor slave to master. He views human beings as friends and coworkers of Ahura Mazda. We are given free choice and intelligence to be responsible for our actions. Just as a flame rises upward, the pursuit of wisdom helps us ascend toward our higher potential. In this journey, there is a mutual relationship between us and the divine. We both need each other to work together in fulfilling our purpose on Earth.

> *For through your own good thoughts, words, and deeds, you shall come closer to the divine. You, O soul, are the one who chooses your own path; it is through your actions that you are guided toward the truth and righteousness. O, Lord of Life and*

---

[26] Gathas: Yasna 33.6

> *Wisdom, I desire a vision of Thee and communion with Thee as a friend.*[27]

"Willpower" is not "will to power"

It's important to differentiate between *willpower* and the *will to power*. The *will to power* is egocentric, rooted in selfishness, and seeks to dominate and control others. It comes from a lack of consciousness and the tendency to identify with our personality. The *will to power* is our struggle to control others, driven by a sense of being special, privileged, or unique. It comes from a deep inferiority complex, a desire for recognition, status, acknowledgment, respect, and control. We seek power because it boosts our ego and nourishes our false identity, much like food nourishes the body. A powerful person may destroy anyone who challenges or questions their ego or self-importance. Power is like a knife. It is neither good nor bad; it depends on whose hand it is in. Is the power held by those who wish to harm and destroy others, or by those who seek to guide and empower others?

---

[27] Gathas: Yasna 33.6

Willpower, on the other hand, is the strength that comes from our true being in charge. It is rooted in inner clarity, with no doubt or hesitation. One knows exactly what they want and acts on it. *Willpower* arises from knowing and seeing clearly. When faced with an obstacle, such as a wall, one doesn't waste time struggling. Instead, they open the door to move forward, making the decision with certainty because they can see the way clearly.

Nietzsche's message that "God is dead" and the call for individuals to choose their own paths through personal choice and *willpower* is often misunderstood and misinterpreted to the concept of *will to power*. Many have mistakenly taken Nietzsche's idea of *willpower* to mean a desire for dominance over others. It has been wrongly assumed that it advocates for the submission and control of those around us. However, this is a profound misreading of his philosophy and what is expressed in *Thus Spoke Zarathustra*.

Rather than advocating for domination or control over others, Nietzsche's *willpower* is about the internal force that drives the individual to overcome their limitations and to become who they truly are. It's the will to live authentically and to shape one's own destiny. It's about self-overcoming and the continuous transformation of the self through conscious choices, wisdom, and courage.

> *With the guidance of the Good Mind, the one who follows the path of truth and righteousness will be led by the divine. The wise will choose their path, guided by wisdom and self-awareness, not by the desires of the self or the ego. The one who chooses correctly will rise toward the higher good and will walk in the light of truth.*[28]

Zarathustra challenges people to ascend from unconsciousness, like animals, to becoming fully conscious human beings. This is the ultimate path toward reaching the state of the perfect, conscious individual—the Übermensch. Zarathustra encourages individuals to transcend their limitations and embrace their fullest potential. The Übermensch represents the ideal person who has fully embraced their own will, guided by wisdom.

---

[28] Gathas: Yasna 32.2

The Übermensch is someone who has achieved human perfection, reaching a state of full consciousness.

Although humans possess the highest level of consciousness on Earth, we have not yet fully realized our complete conscious potential. We still have a long way to go in our journey toward perfection. Our existence has a purpose, from birth to death: to evolve from a lower to a higher being, to transform the Earth into a paradise, and to reach a higher level of wisdom and consciousness toward Mazda-hood. Humans are not born to creep and crawl on Earth like caterpillars. We are born to transform into butterflies—enlightened, conscious beings—to become "the one who possesses the Golden Light."

True *willpower* is an internal process of self-empowerment and self-realization. As one embraces this path, we are aligned with wisdom, not ego and self-interests.

Through Your Good Spirit, O Mazda, guide us in the path of truth and righteousness. May we choose the way of wisdom, acting with purity and courage, For those who walk this path shall be blessed, And through their actions, the world shall be brought closer to the divine.[29]

---

[29] Gathas: Yasna 48.4

CHAPTER 3

Zarathustra's Philosophy

The God Within

The songs in the Gathas are the inner dialogue of Zarathustra with his inner wisdom. He did not see The Sublime Wisdom outside himself, but within. Zarathustra indicated in the Gathas (his sublimed songs) that he experienced Ahura Mazda with his "inner sight." He was one with The Absolute Being.

> *O Lord of Life and Wisdom, when I realized You in my mind, As both the First and the Last of Creation.*[30]

We misunderstand Zarathustra's teachings completely if we reduce them to a dialogue with a being outside of himself. The wisdom he found was through his inner voice

---

[30] Gathas: Yasna 45.8

(*Seraôša*) and inner ears. He was like a diver who searched in the depths of the ocean to find a pearl. He dove into the depths of his own consciousness to find that pearl of wisdom (Mazda) within. The real self is nothing more than Mazda. He encouraged everyone to go into the depth of their own being and to find wisdom (Mazda) in the vastness of their own consciousness.

The Twin Spirits: Unity, Not Duality

Zarathustra speaks of a twin force at work in the world and in human consciousness. The first one is the Good Mind (Spenta Mainyu, The Sacred Wisdom), which wants to pull us to a higher consciousness (Wisdom). This is the force of progression. The other force is called the Wicked Mind (Angra Mainyu, Destructive Force, evil in English). This internal force wants to pull us down to ignorance, destruction, and unconsciousness. This is the spirit of stagnation and deception.

These two forces are not opposite to each other or in a cosmic struggle. They are related to one another as a pair.

In the beginning, there were two primal spirits, Twins, spontaneously active. The choice is given to humans to do the good or the bad, And by their thoughts, words, and deeds, they will shape their destiny.[31]

The best analogy is that of an elastic band. The more one pulls the elastic in one direction, the more another force tries to pull in the opposite direction. We cannot know one force unless we experience the other force.

We don't know darkness if we have not seen light. One thinks that a person born blind lives in darkness. This is not true. Someone who is born blind cannot know darkness since he or she has not yet experienced light. We don't know cold unless we know hot. These two forces are not opposite; they are in relation with each other. They complete each other. They are complementary. We humans grow and learn through our experiences of these two forces, forces that offer us choices. We don't know what is good unless we experience something bad.

---

[31] Gathas: Yasna 30.3

It is through this tension that we gain wisdom. We don't truly understand what is good unless we have experienced something bad. These two forces are not opposites; they are in relation to each other. They complement each other. The contrast between these forces—such as light and darkness, creation and destruction, or order and chaos—pushes us to grow and evolve. Just as the universe itself moves forward through the constant interplay of forces, our personal growth unfolds through the tension between who we are and who we can become. The nature of growth involves navigating this tension between different forces in our lives.

In Nietzsche's philosophy, the idea of war and battles between forces is often mentioned. Nietzsche speaks of a constant struggle between opposing forces, but this is not a literal violent battle between people's superiority and inferiority. Rather, it is a dynamic, vital force that drives the universe forward. It is this tension that leads to growth, transformation, and movement in the world.

In this sense, Nietzsche's concept of struggle aligns with the Gathas, which highlight the eternal tension between forces. This tension is not destructive but necessary for the progression of life and the unfolding of the universe. Just as the universe moves forward through the interaction of opposing forces, we too must evolve through the constant balancing of contradictions. This tension creates transformation, leading to the renewal of our current existence. Without this tension, the entire universe would be in a state of stagnation, lacking growth and movement. Zarathustra calls this state of stagnation *Ahriman* (*Angra Mainyu*).

Ahriman (Evil)

Evil means dullness and emptiness. It does not have a quality. It lacks any quality. Darkness does not have its own substance. It lacks light. Ignorance does not have its own substance. It lacks wisdom and consciousness. It is the state of darkness of the mind. Wisdom is viewed as the light of the mind (enlightenment). Hate does not have its own attribute; it lacks love. Evil, or *Ahriman*, according to Zarathustra, means a state of dullness, stagnation, and lies. Lies mean lack of truth; whatever that is not real. It lacks congruence, authenticity.

Evil is not a person or entity. It is a state of being that lacks light, consciousness, progression, and goodness. It is a state of emptiness and absence of goodness. It does not contain any truth. It is an absolute lie. There is no such thing as a bit of truth or a little lie. A little truth is still a lie—*Ahriman* (lie, *drugh* in Persian). Truth and wisdom represent God (Ahura Mazda), while lies and ignorance represent *Ahriman* (evil), according to Zarathustra. The tension between these two forces—consciousness and deception—pushes us toward growth and self-realization. By facing this struggle, we move from ignorance to understanding in order to reach our full potential.

Hell and Heaven

In Zarathustra's view, hell and heaven are not geographical spaces where one goes after death. The concept is very symbolic. It is a state of mind that one creates for self and others as the result of a person's condition of thoughts, words, and actions. Heaven and hell exist mainly within us. Heaven is the purity of good thoughts, words, and deeds. There is no external punishment of burning in hell forever or being rewarded in heaven.

We all need to understand that our good or evil thoughts, words, and deeds are preparing and shaping our destiny. One always harvests what one sows. We cannot expect to have an orange when we plant an apple tree. Nor can we have a rose flower when we sow weeds. The more wisdom one gains, the greater the person's ability to recognize right from wrong. Wisdom can be defined as the ability to distinguish between good and evil, between right and wrong, truth and lies. Every person must use reason, intuition, and logic so they do not walk blindly. Hell and heaven are the creation that we live based on the choices we make.

> *In truth, the one who shows us the path of truth and happiness in the material world, and saves the soul in the spiritual realm, will attain the highest good. This path is the one that leads us to the true and real world, where Ahura resides.*[32]

---

[32] Gathas: Yasna 43.3

Beyond Good and Evil

And when these Twin Spirits first came together, They created Life and the Denial of Life; And so it shall remain until the end of the world.[33]

These twin forces exist only within the human mind. There is nothing good or bad in the universe. When a tiger kills a deer, it is not an act of evil. It is just an act of nature. When an earthquake destroys a town, it is not because God is punishing the villagers. It happens because of a shift in Earth's crust. People are not inherently bad or evil, based on Zarathustra's teachings. There is no original sin in his teachings.

What we choose makes us who we are and who we become. This is positive, good news; we are not locked into our past behavior or mistakes. We can always change.

Through Your Good Spirit, O Mazda, guide us in the path of truth and righteousness. May we choose the way of wisdom, acting with purity and courage, For those who walk this path shall be blessed, And

---

[33] Gathas: Yasna 30.4

through their actions, the world shall be brought closer to the divine.[34]

The Choice Is Yours

May the people, O Lord of Life, listen to the wise one whose teachings are uplifting and beneficial, and may they follow them in their lives. May they heed the one who spreads the path of truth and speaks with eloquence. Through Thy radiant fire, O Lord of Wisdom, assign the destinies of both the wise and the ignorant.[35]

From the beginning of time, two primal spirits have been spontaneously active in our lives. In thought, word, or deed, one leads toward good and wise, and another toward bad and foolish. Between these two, let the wise choose to be good, not foolish! This idea has been passed along to humanity in many forms. One such story speaks of twin wolves living inside us. One leads us to good thoughts, good words, and good deeds, while the other to

---

34 Gathas: Yasna 48.4
35 Gathas: Yasna 31.19

lies and pain. Which one will win? The one that you decide to feed.

Two Sides of a Coin

Zarathustra teaches us about two forces in human minds (Conscious Mind and Wicked Mind). They're in a complementary position with each other, like two sides of a coin. You cannot take one side of a coin and destroy it and forget about the other side. Both exist together simultaneously.

A man and woman are one soul in two different bodies. They are two sides of the same coin. Night and day are not opposing each other; they're not fighting. Night completes day, and day completes the night. Winter and summer are not fighting with each other. They are moving in a circle and complete each other. This is not dualism. The cosmic battle between these forces and the separation of them from one another are foreign to the teachings of Zarathustra.

Conscience (*Daenâ*): The Inner Morality

The central aim of Zarathustra's guidance is the development of conscience, known as *Daenâ*. According to him, religion is not external but internal. He called it *Daenâ* (conscience). The word *Daenâ (Din)* means religion, which is derived from the Persian word *Didan*, meaning "to see." It signifies perception—to truly see and understand.

The purpose of Zarathustra's morality is the development of conscience (*Daenâ*). "Goodness" is this ability to see (*Didan, Daenâ*—conscience). There is a key distinction between conscience and consciousness:

- Conscience (*Daenâ*) refers to an inner moral compass—the ability to distinguish good from bad, right from wrong.
- Consciousness is pure awareness, free from judgment.

When we engage with our conscience, we can no longer hide from ourselves. The development of conscience happens simultaneously with the growth of consciousness. Zarathustra's ethical teachings are rooted in cultivating *Daenâ* within us. As a person becomes more conscious, their conscience naturally awakens. Such an individual will not act selfishly or harmfully, neither toward themselves nor others. Conscience is our inner sense of truth, our moral values of good and bad, and our innate knowledge of what is just. It is our internal guide for right and wrong.

One acts morally not out of fear, duty, reward, or punishment, but simply because it is the right thing to do. It is important to note that everyone is born with a conscience, but throughout life, we often suppress it. If a person commits a crime, it does not mean they lack a conscience; rather, it means they have buried it deep within themselves, becoming blind to it. Zarathustra does not suggest that people must create a conscience. Instead, he urges us to uncover the conscience already within us and reconnect with it internally.

By elevating our consciousness, we expand our awareness and rediscover our innate morality. It is like an archaeologist unearthing what is already buried beneath the surface. Thus, we do good not out of obligation or external pressure but because our conscience tells us it is right—thus spake Zarathustra.

Our Higher Being

Metaphorically, we touch the ground with our earthly, physical feet, while our head reaches toward the sky—toward our higher being. We connect with the external world through our five senses, but we connect with our higher self through spirit (consciousness). To realize the true self, we must create a distinction between the observer (seer) and the subject of observation (seen). The observer within us is our higher being—Mazda within us. This observer is our essence, the real "I."

Unless we create this inner separation, we cannot grow from our lower, animalistic self to our higher self. This division is known as "inner separation." The work of Mazdaism, as taught by Zarathustra, is inner alchemy—awakening the observer within us until we are fully present and transformed from our lower self into Ahura Mazda.

Human beings are like a circle—there is a center (essence) and a circumference (events). Our center (essence) always remains the same, but people and events come and go in the circumference of our lives. From the moment we wake up in the morning until we sleep, from birth to death, we remain at the center, unchanged by external circumstances. Esoteric teaching is not about changing the self externally; it is about a shift in inner consciousness. This inner transformation is the foundation of Eastern spirituality and psychology.

CHAPTER 4

Übermensch: A Transformation of Humanity Toward Wisdom and Consciousness

Zarathustra descends from the mountains to bring his teachings to humanity. He continues on his way down to the nearby village. Reaching the village, Zarathustra speaks to the people, introducing the idea of the *Übermensch* (Overhuman or Higher Human), a being who surpasses ordinary humanity by creating their own values -conscience (*Daenâ*).

> *And Zarathustra spoke to the people:*
>
> *"I teach you the Overhuman (Übermensch)! Humanity is something that must be surpassed. What have you done to go beyond what you are?*

Every being before you has created something greater than itself. Will you be the one who breaks this chain? Will you choose to turn back and become like beasts instead of striving forward?

What is an ape to a human? A laughingstock, a thing of shame. And just the same, humanity will one day be to the Overhuman—a laughingstock, a thing of shame.

You have climbed from worms to what you are now, yet much of the worm still remains in you. Once, you were apes, and even now, humanity is more ape-like than any of the apes. Even the wisest among you is a contradiction—a mix of nature and illusion. But do I tell you to become illusions or mere plants? No!

I teach you the Overhuman!

The Overhuman is the meaning of the earth! Let your will proclaim: The Overhuman shall be the meaning of the earth!"[36]

---

[36] Friedrich Nietzsche, Thus Spoke Zarathustra

Progressive Mentality (*Vohuman*)

Life is like a river—continuously moving, growing, and evolving. When we reflect on our lives and the past, it often feels like a dream. Existence is like a well, with water continuously flowing from its source. Have you ever felt like life has stopped? Though we may become stagnant, entangled in our thoughts, emotions, or the past, life itself never stops. It keeps flowing.

One of the most important attributes of Ahura Mazda is *Vohuman*—the progressive mind and thought. Every creation begins with a thought, which is why Good Thought is the first ethical principle of Zarathustra, preceding both words and deeds. Our thoughts are the foundation of our actions, so we must always be aware of their nature. Are our thoughts progressive, conscious, and rooted in wisdom? Or are they stagnant, destructive, and misguided?

Good Thought (*Vohuman*) is the driving force behind change, growth, and evolution. This change is eternal and inevitable—everything in the universe is constantly transforming. There is no such thing as simply "being"—

everything is in the process of "becoming." To "be" implies a static existence, but *Vohuman* moves all things toward their fullest potential. Even what appears motionless—like a rock or a table—is, at the molecular level, in constant motion. Nothing is truly at rest; all things flow and change.

> *What is an ape to a human? A laughingstock, a thing of shame. And just the same, humanity will one day be to the Overhuman—a laughingstock, a thing of shame.*
>
> *You have climbed from worms to what you are now, yet much of the worm still remains in you. Once, you were apes, and even now, humanity is more ape-like than any of the apes.*[37]

In this statement, Neitzche is influenced greatly by Zarathustra's fundamental principles of progressive mentality (*Vohuman*). As human beings, we must grow to be a conscious human being (*Übermensch*) and align ourselves with a progressive, conscious life. When our minds are disconnected from the Supreme Mind, we lose our way and fall into deception. But by embracing wisdom

---

37 Ibid

and choosing Good Thought, we align ourselves with the eternal flow of growth, transformation, and truth.

> *Thus I ask You, O Lord of Wisdom: What is Your command for those who seek the truth? May they speak with righteousness and act with a good mind. Through their devotion and just actions, may they bring well-being to all and receive the blessings that come from walking the path of truth.*[38]

In his book, Nietzsche presents Zarathustra as a prophet of radical change, focusing on the importance of inner transformation to realize human potential. He famously writes, *Humanity is a rope suspended between animal and overman—a rope over an abyss. A dangerous crossing, a dangerous on-the-way, a dangerous looking-back, a dangerous shuddering and standing still. What is great about human beings is that they are a bridge, not an end: what is lovable about human beings is that they are a going-over and a going-under.* This passage highlights that human life is a journey of continuous growth and self-overcoming, not a fixed state.

---

[38] Gathas: Yasna 31.6

This is similar to Zarathustra's idea of *Vohuman* - progressive mentality. Life is like a river. It is continuously moving, growing, and evolving. Existence is like a well. The water keeps coming from the source continuously. Good Thought (*Vohuman*) is the progressive mentality and the force behind the change toward growth and evolvement. This change is eternal and permanent. Everything else in the universe keeps changing and evolving except for the change. There is no such thing as simply "being." Everything is always in the process of "becoming." To "be" suggests a state of just existing without change.

Vohuman's force in life drives the world forward, encouraging everything to evolve and grow. We, as humans, must undergo this cosmic transformation, striving to ascend toward the light of consciousness by aligning ourselves with the Supreme Consciousness—Ahura Mazda. This journey reflects the inherent drive toward growth and enlightenment present in both the universe and our own lives. Zarathustra invites us to the need for continuous development and alignment ourselves with higher principles.

Existing vs. Living

It is important to distinguish between existing and living. Everything in the material world exists, but each has its own unique existence, carrying a different degree of life and energy. For example, the existence of a rock is different from that of a flower, a dog, or a human. A rock exists in a state of stillness, with no motion. It occupies space and has mass, but it does not live. In contrast, a flower not only exists but also grows, breathes, and reacts to its environment. However, the life of a flower is still simpler compared to that of a dog. A dog not only exists and lives but also experiences sensations and emotions, forming basic social bonds. It interacts with the world in a way that demonstrates a higher level of awareness than a flower.

In humans, existence is even more complex. We experience sensations and emotions, but beyond that, we possess self-awareness—the ability to think deeply, reflect, and question our purpose. Unlike animals, we can make conscious choices, create meaning in our lives, and seek to understand ourselves and the world on a deeper level. Additionally, humans have a spiritual dimension. Beyond emotions and thoughts, we contemplate the mysteries of existence, our place in the universe, and the nature of life itself.

Existing is merely a basic state of being. It means going through daily routines—surviving, meeting basic needs, and doing what is required without true engagement. It is like being on autopilot, moving through life without a real sense of purpose or excitement. In this state, life happens to us rather than through us. We wake up, go to work, take care of responsibilities, and repeat the same cycle, yet we feel disconnected. We are merely observing our lives instead of truly living them.

Living, on the other hand, means fully embracing life with presence and awareness. It is about being engaged with the world around us and deeply connected to our experiences. When we are truly living, we are not just surviving—we are filled with light and passion. We seek meaning in what we do, find joy, face challenges directly, and build relationships that nourish our being. We acknowledge life's highs and lows but approach them with intention and consciousness.

Elevating this state requires us to raise our vibration by aligning with higher energies such as love, passion, creativity, and consciousness. It means taking charge of our lives and becoming active participants. This transformation involves reconnecting with our deeper purpose, embracing uplifting experiences, and cultivating practices that lead to higher awareness. These practices may include mindfulness, personal growth, spiritual exploration, or creative expression.

When we elevate our energy to a higher level, we begin to feel more connected, alive, and in harmony with the world around us. We become like a plant that is truly living—growing, blooming, and reaching its full potential. We can no longer just exist, merely taking up space. Instead, we strive to live fully, embracing our potential and fulfilling our true purpose as human beings on Earth.

Unlike other forms of life, humans not only exist physically but also possess self-awareness, creativity, and the ability to experience deep emotions and thoughts. Everything in the universe, from a simple rock to a complex human, exists at its own unique level of being.

The complexity and quality of the energy each holds determine its state of existence.

> *May we strive to be like those who guide the world towards progress and perfection.*[39]

Übermensch: A Conscious and Wise Human Being

Evolution is moving from one state of being to another—an ascent to a higher, richer, and more complex form of existence. For humans, this journey is unique. Our evolution is not just about physical changes or survival; it is about expanding our consciousness and transcending our limitations. True human evolution is not solely biological but a transformation of awareness. The force lifts us beyond our basic instincts and material concerns. It is guiding us toward a more conscious and enlightened way of being.

> *What is an ape to a human? A laughingstock, a thing of shame. And just the same, humanity will one day be to*

---

[39] Gathas: Yasna 30.9

> *the Overhuman (Übermensch)—a laughingstock, a thing of shame.*[40]

To reach a higher state of existence, we must awaken and elevate ourselves to a higher human being. A caterpillar can never become a butterfly if it is content to be a caterpillar. This means becoming more conscious of our thoughts, words, and actions. Personal and spiritual growth involve raising our being, shifting from lower, reactive states to higher, more refined levels of consciousness. By freeing ourselves from unconscious behaviors, we align more closely with our true nature and potential as human beings.

> *Man is a rope, stretched between beast and overman—a rope over an abyss. Man is a rope stretched between the animal and Superman—a rope over an abyss. A dangerous crossing, a dangerous journey, a dangerous looking back, a dangerous trembling and pause. What is great in man is that he is a bridge, not an end.*[41]

---

40 Friedrich Nietzsche, Thus Spoke Zarathustra
41 Ibid

Consciousness requires effort. We must be aware of our awareness, staying mindful and present in each moment. It is easy to fall into autopilot during daily routines, but maintaining consciousness means actively protecting our sense of presence. This requires continually returning to the here and now, resisting the pull of distractions and unconscious habits.

Being conscious is like balancing on a tightrope—it demands constant focus and effort. If we lose attention, even for a moment, we risk slipping into unconsciousness, much like falling off the rope. Staying mindful is the key to maintaining our balance, ensuring that we are fully present with each step and aware of our journey.

According to Zarathustra's teachings, we are not born to suffer. Instead, we are here to help make the Earth a paradise, bringing goodness, joy, and harmony into the world. However, our life on Earth is temporary. We are here to grow and expand our consciousness, the part of us that is eternal. Beyond the physical body, there is something within us that "never dies, never gets old, and never gets sick." This part continues even when our time here is over.

Once, someone asked a mystic where he wanted to build his house. The mystic answered, "On a bridge." The people were puzzled and asked, "But how can you live on a bridge with so many people passing by?" The mystic smiled and said, "I want everyone to see my house and remember that life is like a bridge. We are just passing through, not staying forever. Life on Earth is like an airport. We are here for a short time, waiting to catch our next flight."

Our life is like a bridge stretching across a river. This bridge allows us to cross from one side to the other, experiencing the journey along the way. The river represents the flow of life's experiences, emotions, and challenges. While the bridge is essential for crossing, it is not the destination. Just as a bridge helps us travel from one bank to another, our body helps us navigate through life's experiences. It's a temporary container, not our final resting place. The true destination is on the other side of the river, where the spirit can remember itself.

In this journey, the body is like a boat navigating the river of life. It teaches us valuable lessons and helps us grow. Our real essence is beyond the temporary shelter of the boat. On the far side of the river, we reconnect with our true being and the eternal truth within us.

> *When, O Ahura Mazda, I see the order of the world and the wise thought within it, I ask to be shown the path which leads to your presence and to the fulfillment of your will. Guide me to walk upon this path, O Wise One, so that I may help bring about the world's true order in alignment with your will and teachings.*[42]

The Magi

Nietzsche's concept of the *Übermensch* seems to be inspired by Zarathustra's teachings through the followers of Zarathustra (the Magi). The Magi, wise sages and priests in ancient Persia, played a key role in spreading Zarathustra's ideas. Their spiritual and philosophical

---

42 Gathas: Yasna 43:4-5

practices focused on cultivating wisdom, pursuing higher consciousness, and mastering the self.

It's clear that Nietzsche's *Übermensch* is directly connected to the spiritual and philosophical ideals found in Zarathustra's teachings. Both emphasize the transformation of self-consciousness, the rejection of conventional morality, and the pursuit of a higher existence. The Magi seem to have influenced Nietzsche's philosophical reinterpretation of human potential for growth and wisdom.

The Magi were followers of Zarathustra who sought wisdom. In Persian, they were called *moghan*, and in Greek, *magi*. Zoroastrian priests were known as *mobed*, derived from the same root. The Magi were skilled in astrology, cosmology, psychology, meditation, herbology, and alchemy, and they had remarkable healing abilities. The word *magic* comes from *magi*, reflecting their extraordinary power of healing and wisdom. Due to their profound wisdom, the Magi held positions of power in Persian politics.

To find the original meaning of "Magi," scholars look to ancient Iran and the teachings of Zarathustra. He referred to his first group of followers, who sought wisdom through his teachings, as the "Assembly of Magi." These individuals were followers of Mazdaism and Zarathustra. They reached a high level of awareness and were respected as wise leaders who shared Zarathustra's teachings with others. The term "Magi" generally refers to those wise individuals who devoted themselves to Zoroastrian teachings, focusing on self-improvement, spiritual growth, and spreading Zarathustra's wisdom.

> *O, Mazda Ahura, the wise and clever person (magi) is the one who realizes the truth and understands the Lord's Law through their thoughts. They protect the truth and purity with their spiritual power and will speak and act only in accordance with the truth. They shall strive to spread truth wherever they go. Such a person, O Mazda, will be faithful to Thee and will be regarded as the worthiest for helping others.[43]*

In the context of Zoroastrianism, the "Assembly of Magi" could be seen as a group of enlightened individuals

---

43 Gathas: Yasna 31.22

who worked toward advancing both personal and collective wisdom. They were often seen as the spiritual guides, helping others toward a higher state of consciousness.

To truly know ourselves, we must look beyond the surface, much like exploring the depths of an ocean. We need to be like a diver searching for a hidden pearl. To understand our true nature, we must dive deeper and explore the layers beneath—our soul and spirit. Just as the ocean's depths hold secrets, there is a depth within each of us waiting to be discovered. By navigating these inner depths, we uncover the true essence of who we are, revealing the hidden treasures of our being. Just as a flower's true beauty isn't fully visible through a microscope, our deeper selves—our soul and spirit—cannot be fully understood through superficial examination. The real essence of who we are lies beyond physical appearance and must be experienced and explored from within.

Come to me, O greatest Lord of Wisdom, and reveal Yourself, so that my words may reach not only the Assembly of Magians but others as well. O Lord Mazda, guide us and help us understand our responsibilities and the respect we owe to You.[44]

Eternal Recurrence

In addition, Neitzsche's concept of eternal recurrence seems to be influenced by Zarathustra's idea of *Frashokereti*. According to the idea of *Frashokereti*, humanity will go through a dark period where *Ahriman* (the Wicked Spirit) dominates the Earth, spreading lies, deception, corruption, violence, and greed. However, eventually, humanity will awaken to its true nature, embracing "goodness," "wisdom," and "consciousness," and will return to its original, pure state.

Frashokereti means "making wonderful/excellent." It is the notion of a final restoration of the universe to its original perfect creation. The Light will overcome darkness; Truth will win over lies and deception. The world will be reconstructed and governed by wisdom and

---

44 Gathas: Yasna 33.7

consciousness again in perfect unity with the Supreme Being (Ahura Mazda). The world will be restored to its ideal condition.

The concept of Eternal Recurrence suggests that time repeats itself in an infinite loop, constantly returning in the same way. When we observe the universe, we see everything returning to its source in nature. Water evaporates from the sea, forms clouds, turns into rain, and eventually returns to the sea. A forest may burn in a fire, but it regenerates in the future. The seasons cycle each year. The sunrise transforms into a sunset and renews itself as the sunrise again the next day. Everything follows a pattern of return and movement in nature. Human lives are not separate from this cyclical flow. Our lives are also influenced by this repetition, with our past extending into the present and repeating itself in the future.

In the cyclical idea presented in the Gathas by Zarathustra, creation returns to its original perfect condition. This recurrence of the cosmos to its inherent goodness marks the end of linear history. We will once again reexperience paradise on Earth, and our spirits will awaken to the source of wisdom and eternal life in paradise once again.

Figure #3. *Frashokereti* -
A final restoration of the universe to its origin of Paradise (perfection)

Zarathustra's Despair

When Zarathustra finished his first speech to the villagers, the crowd interrupted him with loud laughter and shouting. "Give us this last man, Zarathustra," they shouted. "Make us like these last humans! Then we'll give you the gift of the Übermensch (conscious human beings)!" Everyone cheered and mocked him, laughing at his teachings.

He was forced and threatened to leave the village and the villagers. Feeling sad and rejected by people whom he tried to awaken. He said:

> *They understand me not: I am not the mouth for these ears.*
>
> *Too long, perhaps, have I lived in the mountains; too much have I hearkened unto the brooks and trees: now do I speak unto them as unto the goatherds.*
>
> *Calm is my soul, and clear, like the mountains in the morning. But they think me cold, and a mocker with terrible jests.*
>
> *And now they look at me and laugh: and while they laugh, they hate me too. There is ice in their laughter.*[45]

Zarathustra expresses his sadness with being misunderstood by those around him. He recognizes that

---

45 Friedrich Nietzsche, Thus Spoke Zarathustra

his message is too foreign for them to comprehend, as they fail to see the value of the wisdom he offers. Similar to Neitzsche's story in his book, the prophet Zarathustra also experienced hardship, persecution, and rejections after his enlightenment.

According to Zoroastrian scholar Dhall,[46] Zarathustra, feeling abandoned and with no means of sustenance, turns to Mazda for guidance, crying out as a friend would to help another. With no followers or refuge, he decides to leave his homeland in search of a place where he can fulfill his mission. The people of his town, who have known him since childhood, cannot accept his transformation into a prophet and reject him.

As he journeys from village to village, he faces rejection and isolation. He sleeps in rough conditions, sometimes on the bare ground or in caravanserais, with little food or comfort. Despite the hardships, Zarathustra persists, trusting in Mazda's guidance and finding solace in his

---

46 Dhalla, *History of Zoroastrianism* (New York: Oxford University Press, 1938), 19.

faith, even as he endures physical exhaustion and deprivation.

The prophet Zarathustra expressed his pain and anguish in the Gathas with the following words:

> *To what land shall I turn? Whither shall I turn for protection? My relatives have left me alone and my friends keep themselves apart from me. My co-workers bring me no satisfaction. The rulers of the country are all inclined to untruth. How can I please Thee, O Ahura, by fulfilling my mission.*
>
> *I am well aware, O Mazda, of my inability and insignificant possessions. My wealth is small and my friends and well wishers few in number. To Thee I appeal, O Ahura, like a beloved who expects love, kindness and perfect bliss from his lover. Let me enjoy the might of love and good thought, O my Lord, through Asha, the eternal law of truth and purity.*[47]

The world was not ready for the prophet thousands of years ago. Those he tried to awaken turned against him—

---

47 Gathas: Yasna 46: 1-2

the hypocritical priests, the blind followers of false traditions, and those who feared the light of truth. In the end, Zarathustra was murdered at the age of 77 while meditating, by those who could not embrace his wisdom. His only crime was his love for humanity and his relentless spirit to awaken us from ignorance and deception.

Conclusion

Nietzsche's knowledge of Zarathustra was not based on a fictional character. As mentioned by his sister, he had been fascinated by the prophet from his early childhood and even dreamt about him at times. In his notes, Nietzsche indicated that he had an esoteric and mystical experience while writing *Thus Spoke Zarathustra*. He felt Zarathustra almost possessed him during his walks and experienced a profound mystical transformation as he wrote the book.

Nietzsche studied classical philology, which gave him knowledge of ancient languages. He was familiar with Greek and Latin texts that mentioned Zarathustra, seen as a wise sage. Nietzsche's view of Zarathustra focuses on inner growth, self-awareness, free will, wisdom, and consciousness.

Nietzsche saw Zarathustra as a strong figure who challenged traditional values, just like he did in his life. This inspired him to make Zarathustra the voice of his radical ideas. Through Zarathustra, Nietzsche explored personal transformation and humanity's potential to evolve. He believed individuals must overcome limitations to reach greatness. By using Zarathustra, Nietzsche expressed his vision of human existence reaching its highest potential.

Nietzsche developed the concept of the *Übermensch* (Superhuman) as an ideal individual who transcends traditional morality. He drew this idea from the Magi, followers of Zarathustra's wisdom. The Magi were known for their deep wisdom and elevated consciousness. Nietzsche saw Zarathustra as the messenger of the *Übermensch*, inspiring humanity to evolve. Zarathustra teaches that the *Übermensch* (the Magi) represents the next stage for humanity. It is a goal of self-overcoming to reach a higher state of existence. This involves embracing life, pursuing self-development, and fulfilling humanity's ultimate potential for the good of all beings.

Zarathustra's perspective views life as a journey of progress, where *Vohuman*, the Progressive Spirit, illuminates the Supreme Being (Ahura Mazda). This spirit guides the cosmos toward growth, wisdom, perfection, and goodness, recognizing the inherent dynamism in the universe. The spiritual energy within us is our higher self, like a seed that requires nurturing to grow. For transformation to happen, we must shed our ordinary selves. Just as a snake sheds its old skin, we must free ourselves from the limitations of the lower self. This allows our higher self to grow, reaching the highest level of consciousness, soaring like an eagle into the depths of the sky of our inner being.

Our divine self is like a pearl hidden inside an oyster shell, waiting to be discovered. Just as a pearl takes time to form, our divine self unfolds through inner growth and the effort we put into it. By nurturing and working on ourselves, we gradually uncover the beauty within. This conscious evolution is about transcending the lower aspects of our nature and rising to a higher level of awareness and existence. It involves developing the ability to see beyond appearances, understand deeper truths, and live with a higher purpose.

By embracing this path, we contribute not only to our personal growth but also to the evolution of humanity. It is about creating a world where higher consciousness and deeper connections define our existence. This is the goal of the spiritual journey. This path cannot be handed to us—it must be experienced through inner transformation. Such transformation leads to a deep understanding of our purpose and meaning in life. We are created to master our destiny, but mastery is not freely given. We must earn it through hard work. Just as one cannot be a pilot without effort, we must invest ourselves fully, for this is our true achievement in life.

Humans are not meant to simply exist and crawl on Earth like caterpillars. We are here to transform into butterflies—into enlightened and conscious beings (*Übermensch, Magi*). Without undergoing this transformation, we remain merely sophisticated animals. As we look at the world today, it is clear that we are in desperate need of this higher quality of humanity. Thus Spoke Zarathustra:

> *I teach you the Overhuman (Übermensch)! Humanity is something that must be surpassed. What have you done to go beyond what you are?*
>
> *Every being before you has created something greater than itself. Will you be the one who breaks this chain? Will you choose to turn back and become like beasts instead of striving forward?*

The prophet Zarathustra's mission was to awaken humanity. His aim was to guide people toward wisdom, truth, and inner light. He dreamt of a world where the earth would be transformed into a paradise through consciousness and wisdom. He envisioned a world where people would act with wisdom, not ignorance, and with truth, not deception. His path is an inner journey for those individuals willing to face themselves and discover the seed of wisdom and consciousness within, as taught by Zarathustra and later by the Magi (wise men and women) who followed his teachings. This is the path of those who are followers of wisdom.

Humans are not inherently evil or bad. Our fundamental nature is rooted in goodness. However, we accumulate negative experiences and hardships that can influence us throughout our lives. Our nature is like the sky, and our negativity and wickedness are like dark clouds that temporarily cover it. No matter how dark the clouds may be, the sky remains unchanged. Similarly, we must remove the clouds of darkness to allow the sun of wisdom to shine through and illuminate the goodness within us. We must practice not identifying ourselves with negativity, such as depression, anger, violence, or greed, as these do not define us unless we choose to let them.

We need to align our lives with the realization of human potential, self-awareness, and the elevation of our being toward a higher state of humanity. This is the main purpose of our lives on Earth. Recognizing that we are not fully conscious of our thoughts, words, and actions, it becomes essential to begin with the intention of inner evolution and transformation. It is necessary to cultivate awareness and wisdom within ourselves.

The path of Zarathustra is an inner work. It is a genuine form of psychology and psychotherapy aimed at personal growth and the deepening of wisdom and self-awareness at our core being. It requires a conscious commitment to self-observation in order to develop higher qualities, similar to the Supreme Being, Ahura Mazda. These higher qualities include consciousness, wisdom, peacefulness, love, perfection, willpower, and a progressive mentality.

Zarathustra's concept of true meaning in life isn't primarily about blindly following external moral codes. Instead, it arises from one's conscious inner work and connection to our higher potential. He never imposed "do's" or "don'ts," "shoulds" or "should nots," nor did he prescribe specific disciplines or commandments to follow. Instead, he aimed to offer a glimpse into his own profound inner experience with the Supreme Being. He guided us by helping us understand the origin of his wisdom. Just as geese migrate south to escape the cold of winter, the goal of humanity should be to move toward goodness and wisdom as the ultimate direction of human life, departing from the darkness of ignorance. Since our fundamental nature is grounded in goodness, by aligning ourselves with its wisdom, we find purpose and meaning in our existence, thus spake Zarathustra.

Although Zarathustra was silenced by his enemies for his endless effort to share his wisdom, the spark of fire he ignited has remained alive for thousands of years after him. Like many Zoroastrian fire temples that have burned for centuries despite hardships, the flame of Zarathustra's wisdom still burns in those who have the courage to awaken. His words, his vision, and his truth live on in those who seek wisdom. Friedrich Nietzsche was one such seeker, touched and inspired by the teachings of this enlightened human being. Similar to Zarathustra, Nietzsche's concepts were misunderstood and misrepresented after his death. Unfortunately, it fell into the hands of those blind to his message and the wicked spirits who twisted his ideas. Hope this book has shed some light on their profound wisdom and philosophy.

Darosh Khoh:

May your day be filled with
light, may your path be blessed.

www.zarathustra.ca

www.ingramcontent.com/pod-product-compliance
Lightning Source LLC
Chambersburg PA
CBHW040246010526
44119CB00057B/831